Vortex Street

Heather H. Thomas

FUTURECYCLE PRESS
www.futurecycle.org

Cover artwork, "Satellite photo of stratus cloud fields over the Western Mediterranean Sea, with von Kármán vortex streets to the lee of Corsica and Sardinia," courtesy of the European Organisation for the Exploitation of Meteorological Satellites (copyright 2018 EUMETSAT); cover design by Cecily Moon (www.cecilymoon.net); author photo by Alexandra Whitney; interior book design by Diane Kistner; Adobe Garamond Pro text and titling, Gill Sans sectioning

Library of Congress Control Number: 2018932716

Published by FutureCycle Press
Athens, Georgia, USA

ISBN 978-1-942371-47-2

for Ian

Contents

Because Life Is a Vapor

The Time for Chrysanthemums

Notes
Acknowledgments

The time you call serene descends
Through a moving chaos that never ends.

Wallace Stevens

Double Helix Across the Sky

Postcard from Vortex Street

3/15

Start the day trying
not to hear myself think.
Breath on the page

blows into the street.
Have I gotten over myself
so I can reach you?

Bridge of Letters

When I the upright pronoun
solitary mirrored letter

lay down like a bridge

other letters sang across
the white sky

the brief life you gave me

spun from thread silvery
in the cave of your mouth

an alphabet of leaves
stirred from river's windpipe

where you poured
the flight of birds

ghosts of trees
across the bridge

built letter by letter

of our inked cells
of webs between the slats

trace of you following me
trace of the webs spelled in air.

Slit Silence

The shooting range marked *Danger, No Trespassing,*
    has a target made of old plates.

Shots disturb the birds, ricochet off the ridge,
    separating the air I run through.

In Sarajevo, she timed her run across the bridge
    —fifteen seconds between shots—

the leaves tender on trees not yet burned for fuel.
    Snipers ringing the hills eyed her, eyed

anyone walking home from work or buying bread.
    She counted the seconds on her watch before

running through slit silence, plate of the sun the only
    unbroken thing until she reached the other side.

Room of Not-Knowing

There's a bed, a lamp, a desk,
a drawer spilling its socks. Corners
with the right words for someone

inside a ring of birds,
their laced nests projected
across an inner sky.

When the nests fall from the weight
of their knots, she weaves a screen,
shifts the slant of shadow.

Depending on how she tilts
the bulb, translucence of pearls
or wings of mating dragonflies.

A skeleton dangles her writing hand
from its ear. She hears a name
she once knew,

her own in someone's mouth.
Brief as a negative
held to the light.

Directions to a Skirt Worn by Kit MacDuff Hanging in a Closet in Delray Beach

Going west will only put notions in your head.
Walk east toward the Atlantic.

Cup the sea in your hands and drink.
Now you will find direction.

Remember where your hand met the water.
Place this thought: never panic over a skirt again.

Walk south. All cardinal points are red. Even so,
Kit was a decider: take the skirt and stay insane

or leap to another level. She took the skirt.
Squeezed it into a suitcase she could not lift.

Place this thought in the hotel room:
A filmy blue skirt befits our problems as a nation.

Kit was famous for her wardrobe,
word robe, word rob, even war robe.

War has robbed the world for way too long:
all of history except twenty-four years.

Turn north up the Seagate stairs on Ocean Ave.
Place this thought on the landing:

the gap between the axon of one nerve
and the dendrite of another looks like blue film.

On the second floor kindly ask Veronie
to open Room 279. She will oblige

as this room is now a Florida destination.
The junction where one neuron connects

with another to lay down memories
misfired in Kit. It was leave the skirt or home.

Open the closet and help yourself.

Unhinged

Raw pink pulsing in the storm-door nest, wisps wind-listing
    in the wreath: three blind finches.

Squinched in the twiggy cup, they line up like pins
    unhinged.

Nearly spilling over the edge, the nestlings fill out
    with brown feathers, beaks, fledgling wings.

The storm door opens and closes with the trauma
    of everyday life.

Black-lit beads of their eyes blink like blackstar dots
    on each egg's sky-breath universe.

Why worry how they will make the flight required to live?

Once I plucked from a nest an invasive cowbird egg
    in the tissue-thin shape of all beginnings:

cocoon, womb, ovary, the haunt of roundness we exhaust
    and flee. Now the precipice

edged with droppings stuck to the glass

plunges to concrete. Haunt and the haunting,
    the dead tree in the yard not going anywhere soon.

I wish I was extinct, having used power to destroy.
    The birds lift their heads. Blink. Squirm.

Two pop up and fly off into the magnolia.

The third one, smaller, sprinkled with feather dust,
  sits down. Hours later I open the door.

The little bird hops on the wreath near the fake cardinal
  and takes off. I am out of doors, ecstatically unhinged.

In the empty nest, remnants of eggs that didn't hatch.

Home

Where the tide carves a ledge, wave-thrust dissolves it,
    erasing homes already abandoned.

Sea's steel horizon holds as sand pitches and reels.
    Sunset is a broken conch.

Feet slope and shift into remnants of faults and ages,
    seismic upshots dotted with blue umbrellas.

My arch's channeled whelk around quartz and limestone
    embeds with history forgotten.

Shell-houses brittle and beautiful go home with me,
    as if I could make myself small enough

to live in them. They will pile up in my face-jar transparent
    with cold salt.

The smallest wave inside a person can light or extinguish
    an ember. Nothing but that.

Laying Down the Moon

Last time the water rose
we dismantled
the grandfather clock,
unhooked the iron
weights,
lifted the old moon face,
lugged it all upstairs.
Now with wind upending
the mid-Atlantic
into its howl,
our other moon rests
precarious
against the woodpile,
its crescent tip
tucked between crumbling logs.
We watched this moon
from the kitchen window,
the sky moon gliding
across its mirrored face
filling, emptying, tracing
the arc of an invisible clock
through sheaths of sky.
We walked out back to see
ourselves reflected, to breathe
our smallness into fallen space.
As I slip the tip from the log
and lay down the moon,
I lean over roiling clouds.
My lungs release
something long held.

Orphans

Your light sweeps the field
with the gaze of a fox,

probing night for the gems
of their eyes. Only wild things

fancy you now. You smell deer
before the snort.

Where you lived was not
the place you came alive.

These dead still speak English.
Mother said she'd buy a plot

if I did, too. One day she passed
without knowing me.

You sleep in an abandoned car,
wake under an olive tree,

coat spread on the ground.
Shake the tree—breakfast!

Your father's swift kick
at the exit a road map

to me, promised for life,
though orphans

stay that way.

Postcard from Vortex Street

10/6

Freak October snow
upends ancient oak,

underworld of roots
once ours.

Double Helix

As if heart and lungs flatten back to ribs
    a clearing inside the body. As if there is

no use in a center, you can live
    hollowed out, away from one taking the place

of a mountain, you whose bluff body
    has the power to part water,

to spin parallel wakes, to stand in the way
    of wind's blunt edge, diagonal to the flow.

As if standing at the crossroad
    buttoning your coat, wind-whipped,

the coat scissoring into tatters and you
    spiraling into cloudscript,

a double helix across the sky, the future plunging
    to the past, where friction and pressure

shed a signature
    here, now, on the body vibrating.

A Universe Strewn in Minute Threads

The Fray

*

the fray arcs over the house

     gnarled roots break through ground
     deep down
     they thin to wisps

     the still-growing hair of my ancestors
     twists into a braid

          they link knotty arms

Dear One,

You say the shadow completes its own mark
of abandon. The world outside your door is not houses
or streets. Though you enter the clarity of morning,
your hair blows across your face.

*

what do you hear in this recollection?

    thrum of knots infolding
    a universe strewn in minute threads
    rain dropping through trees
    that never reaches the ground
    in the dark I visualize
    a room illuminated
    with the red glasses
    who drank from them
    around the table
    I crouch beneath
    should I have lifted
    the frayed edges
    my planked eyes
    what did we learn
    that distance did not
    teach in the infinite
    book we read to each other?

*

the difference between lace and paper is nostalgia

> One night our headlights found a saw-whet owl
> silhouetted on the shining blacktop. We thought
> to stop on the wet road, scoop it into our hands,
> its head nearly half the size of its body, like a baby.
> But some part must be mystery, so we drove on.

morning breeze gleams, blows us ahead of ourselves

> a blue scroll unrolls from the ground
> trailing root and filament
> into dry air

> hibiscus opens and drops
> its coral chambers

> even as they intercede for us
> under the elm, even as they wait
> the dead have their own ideas

breathing selvedges of air

    needling beads in my palm I said
    there is the ruffled lake, the trilling breast
    silver stitches strewn across
    the solace of midnight

Dear One,

One day I left the cooking and the washing up
and walked down to the edge of the lake. I got into
the small boat and rowed, a shadow waiting for my
life to begin, green all around me.

a tree branches from both ends

    allotted an inlet of ground
    spelled by memory
    not to have my thread
    cut at a perilous moment

*

only blood between us, many empty years

    when we had words she spoke crescendos
    Chopin, Schubert, summer
    the room was mauve, open
    to the August porch
    she said *his hands flew over the keys*
    his arms stirred the air
    as though memory was the sign
    of loss everything reminded her
    old frayed programs, yellowed lace
    (my history I do not write)
    I was a photograph
    sitting across from her
    we never spoke ourselves

of my gift after this, what is left?

    ghost cloth, a yearning,
    the outline absence makes
    threads down a narrow inlet

    little covers
    hide the fray

*

an unraveled bloom

    riddles the hole
    untangling stray ends
    of mothers and fathers

only one path traverses all parts of the fray

    friction of feet on the wire
    shadow of my mother's hair
    shaken over my brow
    stirs the air, sheen of threads
    twilight binding unbinding
    what is loose and fallen—

Dear One,

Leave the door open, chain up the watchdog,
set out dainty foods. If you rise, the frame will hold.
Inscribed in an utterly woven breath you will be held.

Immunity, I Lost You

Postcard from Vortex Street

4/13

The trees are for you,
the whole of their wideness

blooming magnolia.

Phosphor

Phosphor's trail of eggshells like torn pages
glints in green light on a thought
rehearsed all day:

Saw-whet owl in the moon, a girl on stick legs
slipping down the fire escape
to a blank page

of yard, a sandbox bottle-cool. She flicks
night's neon air, absolving old
romantic tenements.

Her nerves' gold screen spreads its webs,
fastened to her as glints in sand
where she digs

with her hands to establish the work of hands,
herself in that hunting and collecting.
Phosphor reads the illumined

letters she imagines catching hold.
Has he gone for a glass of water
when they vanish

and she flings herself toward frictions
far from his light to cast her own?

The Sunroom

Her legs were shorter then. It's a quick
climb now to the second-floor apartment.

Opening the door, she falls
into the Wedgwood jar of the living room,

a blue world whose patterned white figures
freeze in their dance. Two steps up—

her parents' bedroom—their turbulence
knocks the wind out of her.

I turn and walk as if leaving a stage
Wallace Stevens descended in purple air

more truly and strange, the walls
sliced open by words, so she covers her ears.

The air roars as a plane takes off,
rifling books on the shelves, tearing up paper lives,

rewriting history as snow blowing in
the same bare place between mind and sky,

between sound and night.
This is why the poet is in the sun,

pointing her finger at the moon,
meeting her shadow in a book.

I'm walking room to room with echo
clamor in summer heat.

A line of fire around drawn shades, smell
of burning metal, an overlooked pot,

  but no one has cooked in this kitchen for years.
She crosses the floor stenciled with sun.

I sit on a folding chair and feel the unraveling
in my veins. It's always like this,

  the child not knowing what to do,
how to live. Light over Sixth Street rooftops

leads her down the fire escape to the sandbox
between brick walls until the radio draws her

  back up the iron stairway to the paints,
brush, paper Mother gave her, the glass of water,

the Chordettes singing. She paints a big blue sun,
small ruby bird. Under the covers her page

  glows with ghost letters. She holds
the brush, covers my hand, writing

wayward names that won't go away. Her hand
keeps moving far back all those rooms

  I came through. She writes this.

A Girl, Reading

Mother studies trends in hats.

> *Remember,* she says, *to have style.*
> The straw brim tilts on my crown.

The grandmothers gather into girdles,

> into kid gloves white and black.
> When they argue, I turn translucent

as a photo negative, and open a book.

> *Our sacrifice for beauty,* they say,
> *if only she would cut her hair.*

I memorize everything until I learn to think

> for myself. At the library
> old men in coats stagger in,

sit at oak tables with the *Reading Eagle.*

> Help wanted: hosiery mill knitters.
> Up in the stacks Emma Bovary rots

with desire, Lily Bart loses *The House of Mirth,*

> and Edna Pontellier, shadowed
> by the lovers and the lady in black,

abides the pain of wakefulness. Snug in coats,

> the old men nod heads to their chests.
> My body grows heavy, bones

of my feet chalk blue in the shoe store X-ray.

      Mother says big feet give
      a firm foundation.

At Whitner's department store I stroll

      through Foundations—
      mounds of bras and girdles,

a fresh, white smell.

      A woman in a lab coat dusts jars
      of tinted powders in Cosmetics.

Smoke pours from the stacks at Vanity Fair.

      At Stanley's Bar on Cotton Street
      a man can buy a wafer-thin box

of ladies' nylons, a Polish ham, a Sunshine beer.

      I ride the bus to Fifth and Penn
      and tie fantastic bows at Feel-Fine.

Miss Schultz and Miss LaMonica wear black

      and stand, matriarchs before the racks,
      necks draped with the dreaded tape measure.

My grandmothers depart on the Queen Mary,

      lean on the deck that carries them away.
      No book ever ruined a girl's life, they sing,

waving handkerchiefs. *You'll never know,*

     they sing, as though they knew,
     as though Edna came back

from her final swim, as though my life was not

     a secret ruin of books, secret joy.

Letter My Grandmother Never Sent Me

Had a delightful time with the gentleman in charge of Nash House, Stratford. He knocked down many ripe mulberries from an offshoot of the original mulberry tree in Shakespeare's garden. They were delicious. My first mulberries!

Loved the high spots in Cornwall. Extraordinary fishing villages plunging down to the sea from steep hills fascinate me. Flowers grow riotously everywhere. The majesty of the scenery goes beyond words.

You said *we never spoke ourselves* when we met after all those years. Truthfully, I was in shock from the time you came dressed as a hippie in that long black coat.

Not the girl with half-moon cuticles whose nails I manicured before our lunch of crustless sandwiches. I always remember your little open hand in mine. The room was dark, open to the August porch. Crescendos of Chopin and Schubert.

By then I slept sitting up in my chair so the cancer wouldn't come back. Both breasts and my sex. My wrists were parchment. I tore at the tender spots. Spat at the nurses. *Arrgh,* Arthur wrote that I didn't know how to live. He's the one who died.

Wasn't that years before you were born? True, I was in love with Allan. He got to hanging off the bed, drinking mouthwash. We just went from one lovely spot to another. The snowfall at Lake Louise was enchanting. Such winter beauty I never beheld.

Voyage

Come to her face mirroring sky,
throat swallowing milk clouds.

Come, rosewater and nutmeg
fragrant in tins of shortbread

pricked and scored, wrapped
in clean linen, stowed in the kitchen

where grandfather inscribes her copy
of *Shackleton's Valiant Voyage.*

Come, *mountain* scrawled across her nose
before she slips on the ice and a man in a hat

holds part of her leg. Detached, the retina
makes vision a field crosshatched,

the nerves an ice-scratched window.
She stabs the ice with a pick,

pokes into gray morning,
a portal to proofs inked in blue,

to kickshaws of wax and honey.
As though parts of a body can suggest

what is missing, a child and her father
sing open a spot where the parts

reassemble and walk forward,
carrying themselves.

Letter My Father Never Sent Me

It stinks of decay and something dead here. This place is decadent and morbid in certain ways. It may be beautiful and peaceful, but I like my beauty alive. The other I can understand, but damned if I want to live with it.

All those years you were just across the bridge. You had a new father, new name. Why interfere? How could I, having failed to give your mother a cent?

One day I was flying radar out of Leyte; the next, hoping for a big ship like a C-54, maybe a trade run from New York to Brazil to Africa on up to England and back.

You're going somewhere, and you don't fly yourself into the booby hatch. Which I did, metaphorically speaking, on the 7:17 from Grand Central to Mamaroneck after three martinis.

I couldn't hold still for those ad jobs. Look, there's a war going on. People getting killed by the hundred thousand, guys sweating it out learning life, death and God in the air and in hellholes far worse than New Guinea. And they're learning so they'll never forget.

You get religion in this racket. You get it so you know what it's for. You thank God plenty for letting you sometimes pray a ship in. So when you walk into a church you really see the church for the first time, even though you know God isn't some vast bearded old guy sitting up there on a throne beyond the sky.

I was always happy around water and boats. Nothing holds still except those years on the ship. I would have remembered you then, before you were born. As for airplanes, I am a bit fed up with them.

Look, I can drop in some time. It's easy from here. Try to get some scotch. See if you can get some Canadian ale. Also, see if you can get some salami. I'm nuts about salami and rye bread.

Pagoda

Layers of sirens love this city,
call us to prayer in rush-hour traffic,
the poorest, boarded-up, feared shot
child on the row house porch—

Up Mount Penn to the Pagoda,
fish on the roof protect us from fire,
the tower bell rings, and a poem
takes the place of a mountain.

Across town the air riddles—no,
the air revvs—no, air the texture of trash,
broken glass, flash of a bird wing, a girl's hands
nesting a globe on West Buttonwood.

Look! the murals of marvelous colors,
2nd and Beech, 6th and Greenwich, her billboard eyes
confront my father's ghost—he borrows
a shopping cart from the old Acme—

Who runs this world? His father fights
the Spanish-American War, then works
a hardware store with creak and give
of wooden floors, cold metal smell of tools.

He dies before my father's home from
Army Air Corps spot-jamming enemy radar.
Mechanical stress and fracture split
a sunset cloud above 3rd & Greenwich—

Mother's at her desk fluorescent
in Dick Brothers' basement office near men
fabricating pipefittings and fixtures.
Hat matching lipstick and shoes,

She's typing copy for The Clothes Tree ad,
tracing sketch of a cocktail dress, the figure
drawn with hipbones under fabric,
as Grandfather tallies blast-furnace sales.

The office of furnace and fashion ads
years after the grenade on his desk nearly
kills him at the Somme, but for that can
of bully beef in his breast pocket.

Years before the gentleman my father
steers a pilfered shopping cart of his belongings
to the Guard House bar, now Tropicana.
Who runs this world? We're conjoined

At the head above the eye,
sharing bone and blood, sleeping
with a gun under the pillow,
but no one who knows says a word.

Across town the sun sinks behind
that inkblot, Neversink Mountain. I'm five,
climbing out my parents' window to the fire escape
at the house where Wallace Stevens was born.

Between brick walls, my stamp-sized
sandbox chills with evening and the flash
of neon Foot-Form Shoes where my feet
are X-rayed for corrective boots.

The poet's house now Boylan & Burek
Chiropractic next to Bohio takeout—
I need adjustment. Bundle me backward,
straighten time's spine at the place where

A poet becomes emperor of ice cream
and my parents split. The closed door where
a poem takes the place of a mountain.
Closed door that takes the place of my father.

Moving buttons of light slide over
the Penn Street Bridge, cars like burnt flecks
escaping the furnace as billboard distelfinks
fade behind me on the Reading Beer clock.

Across town my father will be erased.
I will stop being his daughter, become another's
daughter, forget my father until one day
scribbling in my reporter's notebook I remember.

Across town a giant dragonfly hovers
above the hospital roof. Another shooting?
Heart your city, keep it clean, flashes red
above the bridge in a sky threaded indigo rose.

*If we're not able to tolerate each other
we're going to either kill each other, or—*
says Dori, one of Reading's famous conjoined twins,
who changed her name to Reba and then

George, a country-western singer.
Conjoined facing different directions, they see
each other only with mirrors—*I am not this thing
called a conjoined twin,* says Lori.

*I have a soul. I have a heart.
I am one body. I have my legs, my arms.
I am attached to another person because an egg,
the eggs, did not separate.*

The two eggs did not separate.
I'm attached to my father because
his body was conjoined with my mother's
before he was erased and

　　When he died, we did not separate.
I am not this thing a hungry ghost
with my neck as thin as a needle's eye
and my stomach the size of a mountain—

　　Well, leaving is an option, or patience
of a woman cooking *poblano* in her tiny kitchen,
the way Miss Pearl has her morning toast and coffee
looking out the window at 355 N. 2nd

　　Waiting for her ham and yearly bottle
of Black Velvet, cursing Mike for his bender.
He puts up antique Christmas decorations
Pearl had from my father's mother,

　　Along with his Puerto Rican angel
in her crocheted wedding-cake dress.
Now Hogar Crea sells flans for drug rehab
near the library closed for renovations.

　　Across town my son reads and invents
a self-tying shoe. *When I grow up I will be
myself,* he writes. Home creates. A girl
follows the rusty Schuylkill downriver.

　　A woman turns back, curious, drawn
to a web transparent in the light across town
spangling that speck the Pagoda slipping
downward to darkness, as the poet said,

　　on extended wings never her own
until now.

Blue Ruby 3

The day ended
in red sky, blue earth

I walked across
a voice that wished

burning the glass
my father drank from

across the blue
a ruby feeling

printed on my brain—
Immunity, I lost you

naming names
as if my parents

did not lie
together and apart

my fire my prism
as if the searing healed

the sound my own
my radiance

began its walk.

Kindling

A bed in the gloaming holds you
fetal along my spine,
    a glint in the winter woods.

    Wind unspools pine and cone.
You uncurl and stand
    before those traitors, heart and lungs.

    Distance between us filigrees
the impossible seams
    a moment opens: snap of the fallen

    sticks we find. You plant me
in wheelbarrow's bone-cold hold.
    I grip the sides, the cup tilts down:

    softness of mossy floor
turned up by deer.
    Is fear only a jolt from the past,

    separation a fall from the moons
of your arched eyebrows
    to the milky sockets of your eyes?

    Motherless so long to feel
the judgment in all you saw.
    Side by side we sort and lay the bundles

    trembling with a power
they don't know they have.
    The gathering, the wheeling back,

    the stone house raw with its own thicket.
The fire you kindle
    never goes out.

Breathless

You'll never know how cold the wall,
the stone you press on right eye,
left eye, mouth.

You lost your breath, given that words
depended on it. Inside a cave
ghosts negotiate

the issue empty of all you love.
You're not breathing. It's your sister
before she jumps

from Inspiration Point, NY. I know you don't
believe me—*Everything done to you,*
you also did to yourself.

Who is speaking now? Three days frozen,
her body lying there, rescuers digging in.
Your lungs pierced cold

unfold your aunt, the singer silenced
nine years until her mother said,
Get up, go home.

Live your life, care for your daughters.
Her daughter tells the story over coffee.
How does one body contain this?

Because it is not one, and her words
return you to the cave, which spits you out,
breathing again.

Because Life Is a Vapor

Postcard from Vortex Street

7/20

The river's smudged mirror
smells of fish.

Their leaps rope the stars,

the moon,
brilliant in its bowl.

The Same Moon

I am spilled from the house coatless,
carrying the trash. The cold scatters
my face in the dark skeletons of trees.

You're running across the street in your slippers,
singing, "Look up!" and I do, drawn by
the close pairing of bright objects,

Our faces upturned to Venus and Jupiter,
brightest planets, aligned
above a frowning moon.

Turning on the lights in Baghdad,
you studied the same moon,
eight pounds of helmet on your head.

Still you lost more of your hearing.
Starved lions roamed the streets,
forced back into their cages by Bradley tanks,

Filled with assault rifles pointing to the sky.
We could blot out the moon with our thumbs
the way the illusionist refused to show us

The dead. We still have that fire in our hands.

1961

1.

First upside down year.
Ham, the chimp, rockets into space.

Make room for Daddy:
I offer my daughter bread, not a stone.

Registered Chubbette at Lobel's clothing store, she
tries to fathom the Bay of Pigs. New math.

Across the boulevard, new stepsisters.
Through the wall new brother wails

as Freedom Riders cross state lines.
The new dog sleeps in a kitchen cage.

I offer my daughter bread, not a stone.
Do letters add up when stories are forgetting?

2.

Alabama whites ignite a bus, hold shut
the doors with Freedom Riders trapped inside.

She stands before the TV's snarling dogs,
blacks attacked with fire hoses seared in brain for life.

To be hatched instead of born: parthenogenesis,
would that make you free?

I offer my daughter bread, not a stone,
when stories are for getting over.

The new dog sleeps in a kitchen cage.

3.

Our family is a little corporation,
Mother says. *Daddy is the president.*

The President says we are a military-industrial
complex with strategic interests

for preserving markets.
I offer my daughter bread, not a stone.

With Presbyterians, she has debts
instead of trespasses. No gold-leaf vines

twining the lights, no backlit Jesus
hovering in wind-blown robes,

flying toward her from the illumined
window behind the cross.

Vapor

Let's draw the place where you live.
Let's draw the one at home waiting for you,

the food you will eat. Under your desk,
under the wooden library table,

inside the instrument closet,
take this piece of paper, this crayon.

Nurturing healing love, Jesse has written
on the board. Promise me.

Now run outside and keep your eyes shut.

From here on nothing will be like:
I was just thinking, they were just singing,

leaning on each other.

In the time it takes to breathe ten breaths,
to what extent do we actually see or hear?

What is the escape plan for children
between the ages of reason and magic?

Keep looking at me. Because life is a vapor
and days are alphabets. Because the truth

one is not permitted to say.

Omit me, go back in.
Fold your hands on the table.

Let's make maracas from bottles,
tissue, and gourds. Now run outside

and keep your eyes shut. The motion of hope
is not circling alone on a field, gasping for air.

Keep looking at me. Let's try harp of gold.
Here is a shoebox. What else do we need?

Rim of Mountains, Rim of Stars

It started with hate
broadcast on radio and in the arenas,
Sabahudin says. Today an old woman

crosses the square with a basket of roses
and strawberries, ignoring the wild dogs.

On the cold stone of the mosque's
old graves black-and-white cats sleep
under granite cones of hats, the tombs of ego.

Roses painted on streets where a body fell
are being paved over.

Houses crescendo up the hills,
fiery slopes of their roofs unscroll
over long windows, unbroken doors,

as if always this way. Aroma of woodsmoke
mingles with twilight's mauve gauze.

From the city the hillside dots
Of mint, umber, and maize erase
the saturating gray of ruptured concrete,

piles of rubble every few houses the gray
overtaking you and then the white

stones erect on every hillside,
every park a field of chalk, of standing bones.
A woman in the square whispers, *If you have gone*

to the stars you came back because you found
nothing there except, again, yourself.

The call to prayer has a crackling sound,
the rim of mountains ringing Sarajevo
soon to be a rim of stars.

Face of the Earth

In seconds I could have clicked
to the YouTube video,
but the magic turns
when it's played.

Page one of the *New York Post*
was enough: Reporter kneels, stoic

in Guantanamo orange,
throat against the knife,
his face gripped by the
hooded assassin.

End of days, says ISIS.
Our generals say, *Wipe them out.*
Wipe them off the face of the earth.

4:30 a.m. I go outside.
The reporter had the face of the earth.
You have that face.

Oak leaves ink the sky
like hands askew
in their reach and dangle.

I go inside, sit in a chair,
fold over my body,
hang there, dangling my hands.

I get on my knees.

Surely goodness and mercy.
Surely wherever I am
I experience love.

The slow patter of rain
speeds into a downpour.
Flash flood before dawn.

What would Szymborska say?
We made them.

Our weapons their weapons
looted from Iraqi army
after we bombed and
the dictator hid in a hole.

Now desert holes hide ransoms
at GPS points: cash, gas, food, water,
a whole truck dug out of sand.

I devour a quart of ice cream.
Another spoiled American.

I reel when I walk.
Hand over the tinfoil hat.

Then I am back outside,
my face turned up to the deluge.

Then I am back inside,
sleeping with the rain.

Third Eye

My life begins with each inclusion:
feather, fracture, fissure
locked inside the eye,

the iris streaked by every virus—
this is how the diamond grows:

      carbon under heat and pressure
      pushing magma into crystal.

Try to visualize covalent bonding,
stress, cracks, root-like feathers,
scars and abrasions we can't outrun.

      Steps with breath count each inclusion,
      facets invisible millions of years.

Try to visualize a diamond lattice:

      Afghan boys climb a mountain.
      Comes the green flash,

explosive light, the iris streaked

      by every virus *flew high up,*
      and in a second round,

hovered over us, started shooting.

Steps with breath count each inclusion
high in the mountains,

      Pech Valley, Kunar Province.

Scars and abrasions we can't outrun
the forward operations from the base

>named Blessing
>locked inside the eye:

Hemad hit by shrapnel in his side,
hidden by branches that saved his life.

>Because the weather was cold
>and sons went for firewood,

now mothers find their sons in parts.

>Visualize the error in the handoff,

boys misidentified as insurgents
who had attacked the Blessing.

>Scars and abrasions we can't outrun.

Regrettably the boys misidentified.
Regrettably the diamond grows.

>Visualize the *we are deeply sorry,*

the *death, death to America,*
the error in the handoff.

>*Sorry* in the strongest terms.
>*Death* in the strongest terms.

Transform the ignorance or wrongdoing
in my being:

>visualize mothers, boys,
>ignorance, wrongdoing in my being,

how much longer—

spectrum of a wisdom beyond
the diamond, bodies, war after war,

how much longer

      their sons our sons,
      their daughters our daughters,

spectrum of a wisdom beyond.

Aleppo

Hassan, get up

the last drops, the last salt
here on the street

don't let the world see us like this

without water or breath
or anything sung

Hassan, I cannot hear you

night mounts the earth
the father's exhalation

Hassan, they are coming for you

nothing holds together
a few white helmets

don't let them see us

a voice in the key
of desolation

you were an angel to me

at the end of a brightly
burning breath

now I feel I am on fire

Postcard from Vortex Street

4/13

To stay grounded
I follow the map

of your voice
divergent, convergent

and parallel time
as when you arrived

having defeated old ghosts
and stayed.

Found a flashlight and went
looking for them again.

Oblivion

how can you sleep with that train turned up all night

A river of fog runs through the house. I wake to the roar of a train outside the door, and recall another train thundering down the attic stairs, pouring a load of fish into the bedroom. Soon the room is an aquarium filled with fish sprung back to life like sponges.

The train is unloading Haitians after the quake.
Another carries raped Congolese women.
Japanese refugees from radiation are on the way.

Stone faces in my house tell their harrowing stories:

I got out but I lost my wife.
The men forced my son to watch. I never saw him again.
I crawled from a ravine where they'd thrown piles of bodies.

The earth has cracked, shifted, burned. The fuming river across the street glitters with the hiss of gold-mine runoff. Inside, the living room brims with fish and fresh water. Everyone is coming in to eat, drink, live on in the space after I disappear.

Vortex Street

Inhale the mist, hold on to the bridge
    to keep from floating away,

the dusk slit with prisms,
    children chasing fireflies.

Upon entering a drop, light refracts.

*

Braided with wind the river sheds its eddies.
    An old man breathes into balloons.

We think we need to add something:
    time, knowledge, more form,

the past heaped up and hoarded.

*

    A corridor of ashleaf carries me back
to the house of vapors,

    the street moving across the darkness,
the river hidden in fish,

windows filling with trees.

*

You're listening to the bells of empty glasses,
    first one side of the body,

then the other crisscrossing
    the distance between

brocade of the waterfall, phoenix and deer.

*

Downstream by the bridge, a mother gathers
     her children's shoes.

Geese rustle their wings in onrushing spray,
     a sacred geometry:

chains of octahedrons and four oxygens.

*

     We're craning our necks in a vast
cloud chamber

     our bodies rising and crossing
scaffolds of light,

     spinning through eddies, holding on
to air.

Bowl of Oranges

We dared to scrawl our names in chalk.
The beams still bear the marks
across a current of walkways,
map of sticks and apps we made
waiting for ourselves to show up.
Children gathering our bones asked,
Were they dancing bones or sad?
The world never was in place.
How do you want this day to live?
My friend saved a packet of seeds.
The moon illumines a bowl of oranges,
a burrowing owl in desert aquifer,
salutation to rotating oceans.
We were waving not drowning
in the heart's magnetic field.
Imagination is a force: occupy.

The Time for Chrysanthemums

Postcard from Vortex Street

1/15

Waiting for cloud to field
forward into the past.

No wind, only smoke
on sorrow's roof

waiting for window to story
the forest by morning.

No light, only the attic of ice.
If you came, you'd be light,

wouldn't you?

Ribcage

I was inside your hand,
then you let go.

Back to the mines
for evidence of damage.

I kept reaching around
for signs, directions

for transport
into an undamaged

relationship with sky.

(Where were our bodies?

Inside parenthetical ribs,
leaning toward what we loved

that was moving away.)

You were inside my hand,
barely, bracketed

and reaching to draw

your name across
a different sky.

Then I let go, entering
what the ribcage holds.

The Cooling Tower

18 stories above
18 stories below

standing
all those stories

over long-reach river
a ladder welded
to a giant hyperbola

open to sky

wind and water
apart from containment

stamped on the mind
as disaster's icon

a building of melting
uranium rods

nearly destroyed us
years before I knew you

I was walking mid-air
on a tiny platform

18 stories above me
18 stories below

closing in on the shock
of the rim, leaning to peer over

remains intimate with distance

why when I showed how I needed you
did you draw away?

across massive curving walls
the litter of rusted blades, fallen wings

I grabbed the wall and saw
lake of captured water

violet-green swallows
riding the updraft

feet of marble palpitated by salt
face of a medieval weeper

shadow of error, my own
discarded finds

gravity the force defied
a cloud evaporating in open air

so you felt permission to turn away

I was pronouncing from there

a way of being loved

boiled down to a pure drop.

Confession of Belle Scavoir

I left my satin cash
my petal for a paragraph
to grind the gist
his words lit shimmering

around the house at heart
rummage the suffering pockets
to reach the broken
this thought took me away

but form in something else
was not enough
shadow of shapely bottles
now promise one more time

she covered him with a kiss
the sky too blue, the earth too wide
he didn't know the scarlet freight
had bloomed so hard it fell

the river pearled in gray evasion
of its flow, finale of dream
when he slept in his chair

I was a figure of speech
who couldn't undo
another's grammar

and she my love escaped

Caregiver

Breath grabs me from an airless peace,
      my throat a cracked tomb

heaved from a makeshift bed
on the living room rug.

Did I swim the trench zone
      only to rise from the dead?

Did some lifeguard drag me back?
Lungs know the hour they awaken.

I'm scrambling on all fours to the sink.
      When I return, you're there.

It's 3 a.m. You've removed the drooping
roses from the coffee table.

      I put them in the kitchen, you say,
in case you were asthmatic.

You stand before me, wounded eye
and face from last week's fall.

      I dreamed we had a giant
Christmas card with the whole family in it,
you say. *I guess that won't happen this year.*

The woman who always said she never dreamed
offers me a glass of water and

remembers nothing in the morning.

Dorado

Across from our houses the Schuylkill dissolves
      threads trickling from coalbeds,
           flowing into the Delaware,

the Chesapeake, the Atlantic, even without you,
      toward the vortex where it meets
           Old Friend, *Velho Chico,*

the river-sea in Brazil, your other beloved.
      To live along a river means you never stop
           being in the world, yet there's always

a way out. History is a quantum entanglement:
      Are headwaters named for the turtle
           truly separate from the dorado

and women washing clothes in the Rio São Francisco?
      Lilies at Easter, coneflowers, hollyhocks.
           When the hospital claimed you,

orchids. When at last you came home, the Schuylkill
      muddied with rain then clarified as leaflight.
           When twilight came, watery glimmers

lit candles before they bundled in a lamp
      glowing gold inside the river, startling as
           September's chrysanthemums the day you left.

Murmuration

Resonant reverb in my head
when the old woman behind me drops her cane
we're standing in line at Staples
I pick up the cane and hand it back
there are angels walking among us in this world
I catch her gray-glazed eyes
her friend wants to pay for a Pepsi
I'm buying a spiral notebook neon pink
and open the wire-threaded pages
together we fly up to the dome
she doesn't need her cane
by aerodynamics in v-formation
geese save the energy needed to fly alone
red knots and dunlins fly faster
in the wingtip upwash from the bird ahead
we're in each other's murmur
her hand holding mine
our eyes read the starlings'
swoops across the sky
their inky wavings and rorschachs
purplish green-black in the sun

Bowl of Breath

Cumin and quartz on the Golden Horn, bridge across the Bosphorus, brushing Istanbul wind across our faces now dust blown into the shapes we made sitting in the chairs we left behind. On wet stone slabs we stretch like cats before the singing with the scrub under light through the dome's chiseled stars. Wind rustles silver olive trees. Night-flute plays with dogs and a rooster until *al-salaatu khayrun min al-nawm:* praying is better than sleeping. Staff of Moses, saucepan of Abraham, dust from prophets collected in a bowl. Saints with their eyes rubbed out, restored, rubbed out again in Cappadocia's cave church, our breath melting the frescoes. A diamond in a dump heap sold to a peddler for three spoons. The tree of life in a bowl for your son. Holy water from Mary's spring. How many knots do you make as a flower in the fire? Must you shake the palm to know the dates, the hands opening and closing, the bowl uplifted spilling water on your head, waking the light? Be like the sea in tolerance. Either exist as you are or be as you look. Streaming out in a fog. Changed coming back.

Dark-Mapping toward Tanta

      Outside the night airport, dust hangs
its fabric scissored by murmurs, horns, barks,
smoky aroma of shisha and meat

rising above the trash no one wants
to remember, or forget.

      A self I left at home remembers and forgets
in rackets of space split by distractions,
guns every day in the news,

as if a world can be made
from a brother's murder.

      Cars speeding out of Cairo zigzag
invisible lanes, the horns relentless
as the missing,

as fear dismantling in the flash
that conjures lifeline. I dark-map it

      in the back seat with pen and paper:
dust's luster the veil that lifts by morning,
the Sea of Sand afloat in air

where water has memory
and the moon is sung by a boy.

Your Arabic, Your Hebrew

Alive with you
something would return me

let my life speak
something in your stroke

recumbent in the thicket
of my cursive

I climbed up
lay across your languages

pillars with capitals
I had no idea how to read

birds flying backward
swoop and wave

your calligraphy
I would transcribe

listening through walls
who was there

incomprehensible
trusting the other in myself

I traveled to meet you.

Atonement

Which one travels
toward the stranger?

Who in nightspeed slits
of borders, time zones

word-maps crossing
multilingual

what's on the tongue
risking trust

without translation
atonement in a zip of light

drawn across the sky's
at(one)ment

as the light shifts
but does not separate

one with other, one.

Marathon

In the room of not-knowing,
you are texting, thumbs fluttering
in your lap like butterflies

until I mark you absent
because there are no butterflies here.
Text is now a verb like *like*.

Kitchen pots used for bombs!
Crystal exclaims from the corner,
scanning her iPad amid

"A Ritual to Read to Each Other."
The world's a broken bell jar.
A rabbit will be king of the ghosts.

Three days' fever washed out of my hair,
I'm about to reveal the difference
between *lightning* and a *lightning bug,*

between logical and ethical appeals.
Despite the bombing in Boston,
this is not quaint. This is not

an academic exercise. This is King
writing his *Letter from Birmingham Jail*
and my lesson against forgetting.

Each day it breaks through
the cocoons before me as you
who are writing down your lives

on the bomb of an alien god.
To climb out of the craters
and the hate they contain

with the same hands that move
a pen. In your taps on the screen
I hear the rush of wings opening.

Chrysanthemums

I'm walking from the house of my earliest dreams,
a rememberer mouthing the flowers,

mistaking what I loved for what I lost,
unable to leave until water writes across my face.

Must I make amends before asking will the next life
be better than this one?

Now together we will give up every minute.
Why speak when silence is more appropriate?

Now I will unravel the knots of our breath,
as if the problem of living could be lifted and carried

away from the dream of our talks,
your story on the page I was divinely charged

to rewrite from the park bench where the book
lay open on your lap.

Why insist on my life when my body is not
mine alone but also contains yours,

this body that carried me to your door,
arms raised to reach or to shield myself from you

who might hold me for a second in this world
where history is always ready to get worse.

What I remember is the time for chrysanthemums.
Now I can't plant enough of them.

Risk

Why the less safe, the more true? My life tapped out on Mother's mahogany table next to my wall of books. Today for no reason the sun rose, the trees windless in their green. The grass is not a lake. I'm always into something like a landscape. If I could write it and also write about it. With memory the Balanced Rock sits on pinnacle's edge through wind, water, and ice in vistas shear-shaped over eons. The hoodoos silent as we switchback below them. As if here always exactly. Betrayal only in the stones I gather. The centuries collapse through each other like floors in a burning building until we get to this moment when water bursts through the wall of my bookshelves, scattering works of the authors who carried me through. What can this space hold but the hollow core as promise, light that protects as it pushes away?

Notes

Vortex Street: A repeating pattern of swirling vortices formed in clouds or water in the wake of an obstacle. A phenomenon of fluid dynamics.

"Double Helix": A "bluff body" is an obstacle, such as an island, on a vortex street. It interrupts the elemental path and makes a spiraling wake that resembles the chain of a double helix.

"The Sunroom" is indebted to Wallace Stevens, born at 323 North Fifth Street, Reading, Pennsylvania, a house where I resided briefly as a child.

"Phosphor" is after Wallace Stevens's "Phosphor Reading by His Own Light."

"Voyage" responds to Magritte's painting "L'Évidence Eternelle."

"Pagoda" refers to a national landmark atop Mount Penn in Reading, Pennsylvania. The conjoined twins Lori and Dori Schappell, born in Reading in 1961, achieved notoriety through Dori's pursuit of a singing career. As a mark of individuality, and disliking the fact that their names rhymed, Dori at first went by Reba, and then changed her name to George. Their quotes are from a 2005 BBC report, "Sisters' Hope: Conjoined Twins."

"Face of the Earth" is in memoriam for journalist James Foley, who was murdered by ISIS on August 19, 2014, near Raqqa, Syria.

"The Same Moon" is for Bridget Cummings Niehus.

The epigraph in "Oblivion" is from "The White of Action in Literature" by Brenda Hillman.

"The Cooling Tower" refers to the Three Mile Island nuclear power plant, site of the worst commercial nuclear power plant accident in U.S. history on March 28, 1979. The island is in Pennsylvania's Susquehanna River, a Native American name with meanings that include "long-reach river."

"Confessions of Belle Scavoir" is indebted to "Bouquet of Belle Scavoir" by Wallace Stevens. "Satin cash" is from Emily Dickinson.

"Dorado" is in memoriam for Elizabeth Kiddy.

"Atonement" is indebted to Barnett Newman's painting, "Onement, I."

Acknowledgments

Grateful acknowledgment to the editors of the print and online publications where these poems or earlier versions first appeared:

About Place Journal: "Postcard from Vortex Street"
Barrow Street: "Double Helix"
Canadian Woman Studies: "Blue Ruby 3"
Diogen: Pro Kultura (Sarajevo): "Vortex Street," "Postcards from Vortex Street"
Ëndërr E Shituar (Tetovë, Macedonia): "Slit of Silence"
Ekphrasis: "Bowl of Breath"
Excavating Honesty: An Anthology of Rage and Hope in America: "Marathon"
Fledgling Rag: "1961," "Laying Down the Moon," "Marathon," and "Oblivion"
The Fray: A 12-page poem-embroidery collaboration with artist Barbara Schulman
Hesham Alsabahi's Poetry Book Blog (Arabic): "Blue Ruby 3," "Postcard from Vortex Street," "Slit Silence," "Bridge of Letters," "Ribcage," "Bowl of Breath," "Caregiver"
The Historical Review of Berks County: "Pagoda"
Interim: "Third Eye"
Liberty's Vigil, The Occupy Anthology: "Postcard from Vortex Street"
Merkurius: "Room of Not-Knowing," "Vortex Street," "Slit Silence"
Minerva Online: "Ribcage," "Chrysanthemums," "Blue Ruby 3"
Oír Ese Río (Hear That River): "Dorado"
The Pedestal Magazine: "Vapor"
Poems for the Writing: Prompts for Poets: "Letter My Father Never Sent" and "Letter My Grandmother Never Sent"
Poetry24: "Face of the Earth"
Poezijos Pavasaris 2013 (Vilnius): "Rim of Mountains, Rim of Stars," "Slit of Silence," "Vapor," "Letter My Father Never Sent Me"
Press 1: "Room of Not-Knowing" and "Directions to a Skirt Worn by Kit MacDuff Hanging in a Closet in Delray Beach"
Tanta International Festival of Poetry Anthology: "Slit of Silence"

Talisman: A Journal of Contemporary Poetry and Poetics: "Vortex
    Street" and "Postcards from Vortex Street"
The Wallace Stevens Journal: "The Sunroom"
Women's Studies Quarterly: "Home"

I am grateful to the Salem College Center for Women Writers for
awarding "Slit Silence" the Rita Dove Honorable Mention Poetry
Prize, 2014 International Literary Awards. My thanks to the Virginia
Center for the Creative Arts for a fellowship that provided time and
space to begin this project.

Deep and abiding thanks to Lawrence Bridges, Kristina Marie
Darling, Barbara Presnell, Lisa Sewell, and J. C. Todd for your gen-
erous words about these poems. For readings, encouragement, and
suggestions at pivotal moments, I thank Laure-Anne Bosselaar, Lisa
DeVuono, Sandra Fees, Carolyn Forché, Susan Kerschner, Deanna
Ludwin, Bridget Cummings Niehus, Lisa Norris, Daniel T. O'Hara,
Barbara Presnell, Beth Seetch, Catherine M. Soussloff, Billie Travalini,
and the late C. D. Wright. I am grateful to my translators Marius
Burokas, Vendela Engblom, Diti Ronen, Fatima Tahir, Elvana Zaimi-
Tufa, and Sabahudin Hadžialić. Always, Craig Czury.

Abiding gratitude to Cecily Moon for her beautiful cover design and
support of my work over many years. Deepest thanks to my publisher
Diane Kistner and the editors at FutureCycle Press for believing in my
work and bringing this book to print.

About FutureCycle Press

FutureCycle Press is dedicated to publishing lasting English-language poetry books, chapbooks, and anthologies in both print-on-demand and Kindle ebook formats. Founded in 2007 by long-time independent editor/publishers and partners Diane Kistner and Robert S. King, the press incorporated as a nonprofit in 2012. A number of our editors are distinguished poets and writers in their own right, and we have been actively involved in the small press movement going back to the early seventies.

The FutureCycle Poetry Book Prize and honorarium is awarded annually for the best full-length volume of poetry we publish in a calendar year. Introduced in 2013, our Good Works projects are anthologies devoted to issues of universal significance, with all proceeds donated to a related worthy cause. Our Selected Poems series highlights contemporary poets with a substantial body of work to their credit; with this series we strive to resurrect work that has had limited distribution and is now out of print.

We are dedicated to giving all of the authors we publish the care their work deserves, making our catalog of titles the most diverse and distinguished it can be, and paying forward any earnings to fund more great books.

We've learned a few things about independent publishing over the years. We've also evolved a unique, resilient publishing model that allows us to focus mainly on vetting and preserving for posterity poetry collections of exceptional quality without becoming overwhelmed with bookkeeping and mailing, fundraising activities, or taxing editorial and production "bubbles." To find out more about what we are doing, come see us at www.futurecycle.org.

The FutureCycle Poetry Book Prize

All full-length volumes of poetry published by FutureCycle Press in a given calendar year are considered for the annual FutureCycle Poetry Book Prize. This allows us to consider each submission on its own merits, outside of the context of a contest. Too, the judges see the finished book, which will have benefitted from the beautiful book design and strong editorial gloss we are famous for.

The book ranked the best in judging is announced as the prize-winner in the subsequent year. There is no fixed monetary award; instead, the winning poet receives an honorarium of 20% of the total net royalties from all poetry books and chapbooks the press sold online in the year the winning book was published. The winner is also accorded the honor of being on the panel of judges for the next year's competition; all judges receive copies of all contending books to keep for their personal library.

www.ingramcontent.com/pod-product-compliance
Lightning Source LLC
Chambersburg PA
CBHW070007100426
42741CB00012B/3138